WASHINGTON, D.C.

WASHINGTON, D.C.

HELLO U.S.A.

by Joyce Johnston

Lerner Publications Company

You'll find this picture of cherry blossoms at the beginning of each chapter. The cherry trees that grow these flowers were a gift to the United States from Japan. Cherry trees bloom in the spring, producing clusters of beautiful pink and white blossoms. Washingtonians celebrate the trees each year at the Cherry Blossom Festival.

Cover (left): The Washington Monument. Cover (right): The White House. Pages 2–3: The U.S. Capitol building. Page 3: The statue of Lincoln inside the Lincoln Memorial.

Copyright © 2003 by Lerner Publications Company

This book is available in two editions:
Library binding by Lerner Publications Company, a division of Lerner Publishing Group
Soft cover by First Avenue Editions, an imprint of Lerner Publishing Group
241 First Avenue North
Minneapolis, MN 55401 U.S.A.

Website address: www.lernerbooks.com

Library of Congress Cataloging-in-Publication Data

Johnston, Joyce, 1958–
    Washington, D.C. / by Joyce Johnston (Rev. and expanded 2nd ed.)
        p.   cm. — (Hello U.S.A.)
    Includes bibliographical references and index.
    Contents—The land: more than a city—The history: changing with the nation—People and economy: U.S.A. headquarters—The environment: the war on CFCs—All about Washington, D.C.—Fun facts—Official song—A Washington, D.C., recipe—Historical timeline—Outstanding Washingtonians—Facts-at-a-glance—Major parks and gardens—Places to visit—Annual events—Learn more about Washington, D.C.
    ISBN: 0–8225–4091–6 (lib. bdg. : alk paper)
    ISBN: 0–8225–0798–6 (pbk. : alk paper)
    1. Washington (D.C.)—Juvenile literature. [1. Washington (D.C.)] I. Title. II. Series.
F194.3.J64 2003
975.3—dc21   2001008655

Manufactured in the United States of America
 2 3 4 5 6 – JR – 08 07 06 05 04 03

CONTENTS

Cherry trees, originally sent from Japan, line a large pool called the Tidal Basin. The Jefferson Memorial can be seen in the background.

THE LAND

More Than a City

ashington, D.C., the capital of the United States of America, is located on the nation's East Coast, about 150 miles from the Atlantic Ocean. The city sits on the Potomac River, between the states of Maryland and Virginia. Washington is the headquarters of the U.S. government. The U.S. Congress meets there, the president lives and works there, and citizens from around the nation come there to express their opinions.

Washington, D.C., is not part of any state. It belongs to a separate district, or section, of the United States. Named after explorer Christopher Columbus, this section is called the District of Columbia (or D.C.). The district covers 68 square miles. The city of Washington and the District of Columbia cover the exact same area.

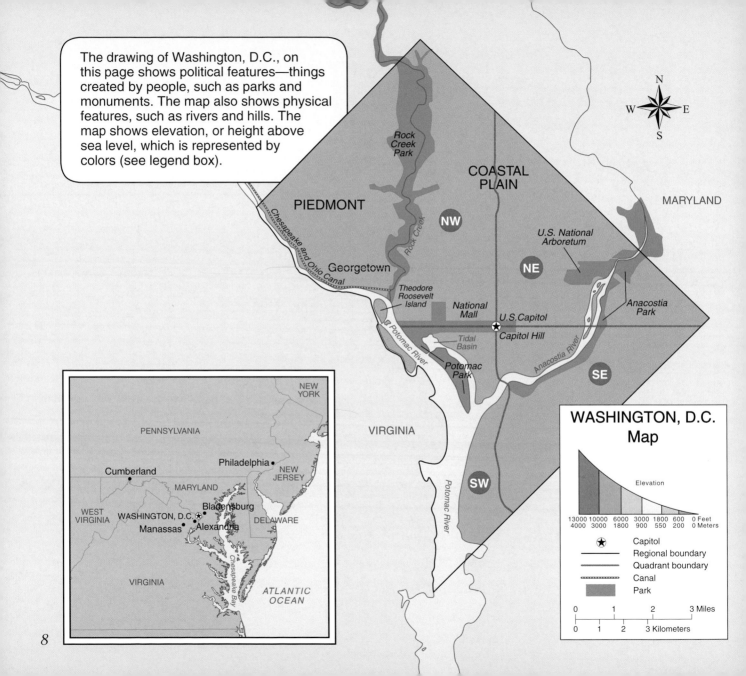

The drawing of Washington, D.C., on this page shows political features—things created by people, such as parks and monuments. The map also shows physical features, such as rivers and hills. The map shows elevation, or height above sea level, which is represented by colors (see legend box).

Rock Creek Park

COASTAL PLAIN

PIEDMONT

MARYLAND

NW

U.S. National Arboretum

NE

Chesapeake and Ohio Canal

Georgetown

Theodore Roosevelt Island

National Mall

U.S. Capitol

Anacostia Park

Rock Creek

Capitol Hill

Tidal Basin

Potomac River

Potomac Park

Anacostia River

SE

VIRGINIA

SW

Potomac River

WASHINGTON, D.C. Map

Elevation

| 13000 | 10000 | 6000 | 3000 | 1800 | 600 | 0 Feet |
| 4000 | 3000 | 1800 | 900 | 550 | 200 | 0 Meters |

★ Capitol

Regional boundary

Quadrant boundary

Canal

Park

| 0 | 1 | 2 | 3 Miles |

| 0 | 1 | 2 | 3 Kilometers |

Inset map

NEW YORK

PENNSYLVANIA

Cumberland

Philadelphia

NEW JERSEY

MARYLAND

Bladensburg

WEST VIRGINIA

WASHINGTON, D.C.

DELAWARE

Manassas

Alexandria

VIRGINIA

Chesapeake Bay

ATLANTIC OCEAN

8

Maryland is Washington's neighbor to the north, east, and southeast. To the southwest, across the Potomac River, lies the state of Virginia. Washington's suburbs extend far into Maryland and Virginia. The Washington, D.C., metropolitan area—the city and all its suburbs—covers 3,957 square miles, more than 50 times the size of the city itself.

The city of Washington is divided into four parts—Southeast, Southwest, Northeast, and Northwest. These four sections meet at the U.S. Capitol building, which sits on a hill close to the Potomac River. Known as Capitol Hill, the hill is also the site of the Supreme Court, the Library of Congress, and other important government buildings.

Senators and representatives meet in the Capitol building to make laws for the United States.

9

The Federal Triangle is formed by the Washington Monument *(tall column at center),* the Capitol *(large dome at far left),* and the White House *(not shown).*

Washington was a planned city, designed by Pierre Charles L'Enfant, a French engineer and architect. He situated the president's house, called the White House, about 1.5 miles northwest of the Capitol

The Lincoln Memorial, with its tall, white columns, can be seen above at left, and the domed roof of the Jefferson Memorial is at far right.

building. Between the White House and the Capitol, he placed the Federal Triangle, which has more government buildings than any other place in the city.

Washington has lots of public parks, many of which contain sculptures and other works of art.

Parks were an important part of L'Enfant's plan. One park, called the National Mall, stretches two miles from the Capitol building to the Lincoln Memorial. Other large city parks include Potomac Park, Rock Creek Park, and Anacostia Park.

Washington's metropolitan area spreads across two geographic regions—the Coastal Plain and the Piedmont. Most of the city sits on the low-lying Coastal Plain, which extends east to the Atlantic Ocean. The western edge of the city, plus the western suburbs, sits on the higher land of the Piedmont. Rock Creek, a small stream that flows through western Washington, separates the Coastal Plain from the Piedmont.

Where the Piedmont meets the lower Coastal Plain, rushing waterfalls form on the Potomac River.

The rock of the Piedmont is harder than that of the Coastal Plain. Upstream from the Georgetown neighborhood, the Potomac River has been able to carve only a narrow channel through the Piedmont's hard granite. Downstream, the river has cut a wide path through the soft earth of the Coastal Plain.

Two major rivers flow through Washington. One is the Potomac, which flows east into Chesapeake Bay. The other river, the Anacostia, flows south from Maryland and meets up with the Potomac at the tip of Potomac Park.

Washington's climate is mild and moist. About 50 inches of **precipitation** (rain, snow, sleet, and hail) fall on the city each year. The average temperature in winter is 37° F. In summer the average temperature is 78° F, but it's not unusual for temperatures to rise above 90° F on a July or August afternoon.

With its warm weather, Washington is a good home for many different plants, including cherry trees in Potomac Park. A gift from Japan, the trees produce thousands of delicate pink and white blossoms every April.

Other trees and shrubs from around the world thrive in the National Arboretum, a special park where scientists can study plants. The arboretum is well known for its herb garden, its collection of bonsai plants (miniature potted trees), and its flowering azalea shrubs.

Colorful dogwoods and azaleas brighten Washington's National Arboretum.

Washington's parks provide homes for bullfrogs and other small animals.

Animals such as gray and red squirrels, cottontail rabbits, woodchucks, muskrats, and chipmunks all make their homes in Washington's parks and natural areas. Visitors might also hear bullfrogs or cricket frogs in the parks, or see a salamander slither across a rock. Bird-watchers in Washington enjoy finches, scarlet tanagers, warblers, and wood thrushes. Washington's rivers are home to fish such as bass, catfish, shad, and sunfish.

Changing with the Nation

 ong before Washington became the capital of the United States, thousands of Native Americans, or American Indians, lived in the area. The Nanticoke, Piscataway, and Powhatan Indians fished in the waters of the Potomac River and the Chesapeake Bay.

Starting in the early 1600s, English settlers began to arrive in North America. They gradually took over lands along the East Coast, forcing the Indians to move west and north. The settlers also brought smallpox and other diseases from Europe. Thousands of Native Americans died from these illnesses.

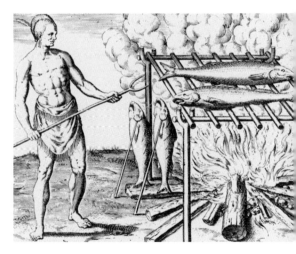

Powhatan Indians fished in the Potomac. They preserved their catch by drying it over a fire.

The English settlers established towns and farms in Maryland, Virginia, and other places along the Atlantic Ocean. Eventually, the settlers broke their ties with England. They established an independent nation, the United States of America. In 1789 George Washington became the first president of the United States.

The new nation needed a permanent capital city. Several states offered to donate land for a capital. But Congress, the group of people elected to make laws for the country, could not decide whether the capital should be located in a northern or a southern state. Because the capital would be such an important city, people from each region wanted to have it in their area.

The city of Washington was named after the nation's first president, George Washington.

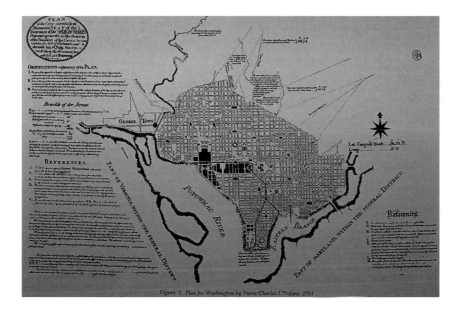

Figure 9. Plan for Washington by Pierre Charles L'Enfant: 1791

A French engineer named Pierre Charles L'Enfant designed Washington, D.C., in 1791. He placed the Capitol building in the center of the city.

In 1790 Congress reached a compromise. It would locate the capital on the Potomac River—a southern location. In exchange, congressmen from the South agreed to support some laws favored by the North.

Congress asked President Washington to pick the capital's exact location. He chose 10 square miles of land straddling the Potomac between Maryland and Virginia, about 75 miles inland from Chesapeake Bay. The new capital city was named Washington, after the president.

In the 1790s, farmers lived in the area that would become the District of Columbia.

The site of the future city contained forests, swamps, fields of corn and tobacco, and two small towns—Alexandria in Virginia and Georgetown in Maryland. The site was home to white farmers and townspeople. By then all the Indians in the area had died of illness or had been forced off their lands.

In 1800 the U.S. government moved to Washington from a temporary capital in Philadelphia. A few government buildings had been constructed, but the rest of Washington was a mess. The streets were not paved. They were filled with potholes and tree stumps, which made travel dangerous. In dry weather, the dirt roads turned dusty, and dust filled the air. In rainy weather, the roads turned to mud. Residents often dumped garbage into the streets. Farmers let pigs and other animals roam through the city. The capital was so rough and dirty that it was sometimes called Wilderness City.

In the early 1800s, farm animals freely wandered the streets of Washington, D.C.

In 1812 the United States declared war on Great Britain. Great Britain had been fighting France for more than 10 years and was trying to prevent other countries, including the United States, from trading with the French. British ships had been stopping U.S. trading ships on the Atlantic Ocean and forcing U.S. sailors to join the British navy. The conflict became known as the War of 1812.

On August 24, 1814, the British attacked Bladensburg, Maryland, northeast of Washington.

British sailors would capture American seamen and force them to join the British navy. Called impressment, this practice was one of the causes of the War of 1812.

22

In less than an hour, the British had defeated the U.S. soldiers. The Americans fled so quickly that the battle became known as the Bladensburg Races.

British soldiers then marched into Washington and set fire to the Capitol and the president's house. They destroyed the bridge over the Potomac River, and the War and Treasury Department buildings.

British troops set fire to many of Washington's buildings during the War of 1812.

23

Before the slave trade was abolished in Washington, traders kept slaves in buildings like this one.

Because the British ruined nearly all the government buildings in Washington, residents were afraid Congress would move the capital someplace else. But in February 1815, Congress voted to stay and rebuild the city. That same month, President James Madison signed a **treaty** with the British, ending the War of 1812.

By 1820 Washington had become a slave-trading center. Slavery was common in the United States, mainly in the South. Slaves were African Americans who had been captured in Africa or were born into slavery in the United States. In Washington, slave traders kept slaves in city jails and in pens set up along the National Mall.

Many people, particularly Northerners, thought slavery was wrong. These **abolitionists** asked Congress to make the slave trade illegal in Washington. Abolitionists felt ashamed that people were bought and sold in the capital of a nation that claimed to give freedom to everyone. In 1850 Congress outlawed the slave trade in Washington.

The Nation's Attic

When British scientist James Smithson died in 1829, he left his fortune to the United States. Smithson wanted the U.S. government to use his gift to build a scientific institution that would increase and spread knowledge. In 1846 Congress created the Smithsonian Institution. Since then, the Smithsonian has been involved in many areas of study.

In the late 1800s, the institution helped pay for expeditions to western North America. Explorers returned with animals they had caught and stuffed. Many explorers also brought back baskets, pottery, and other items made by Native Americans. These things became part of the Smithsonian's collection.

In modern times, the Smithsonian Institution is best known for its museums, several of which line the National Mall. Visitors to the museums can see everything from the Hope diamond—one of the world's most valuable diamonds—to the very first phones made by Alexander Graham Bell.

The museums also display paintings, sculptures, clothing, weapons, airplanes, books, space capsules, and prehistoric animal skeletons. Although millions of items are on display, only 1 percent of everything the Smithsonian owns can be shown at one time. With the country's past stored in its warehouses, the Smithsonian has come to be known as the Nation's Attic.

The Smithsonian Institution Building

Union troops camped close to Washington, D.C., during the Civil War. Families sometimes visited soldiers in camp.

By 1861 the Northern states had outlawed slavery, while slavery remained legal in the South. When Abraham Lincoln became president, Southern leaders worried that the United States would outlaw slavery in all states. After Lincoln's election, 11 Southern states formed their own nation, called the Confederate States of America, or the Confederacy. To preserve the United States, President Lincoln led the Union (Northern) army against the Confederate army. The conflict became known as the Civil War. Washington, D.C., sided with the Union.

One of the first important battles of the Civil War took place in July 1861, about 30 miles from the District of Columbia near Manassas, Virginia. Washingtonians were sure that the Northern army would win the battle quickly. Many residents even took picnic lunches to watch the fight.

Union troops camped close to Washington, D.C., during the Civil War. Families sometimes visited soldiers in camp.

But the Northern army lost the battle. Wounded men walked or were carried in carts back to Washington. People there cared for the wounded soldiers in homes, schools, churches, and government offices. Doctors treated some soldiers in the Capitol building itself.

Washington's population grew rapidly during the war. Many people came to the city to start new businesses or to take government jobs related to the war. Thousands of slaves fled Confederate states and settled in Washington, where slavery was outlawed in 1862.

The North won the war in 1865, and slavery was made illegal throughout the United States. That same year, Congress gave African American men the right to vote in the District of Columbia. In 1868 Washington residents elected John F. Cook and Carter A. Stewart to the city council. They were the first African Americans to hold public office in the nation's capital.

Over the years, the Capitol building has been restored and expanded. Its dome was added in 1865.

By the early 1900s, Washington was a bustling city *(right)*. But many African Americans *(below)* had difficulty finding good jobs.

At the beginning of the 1900s, Washington was a bustling city. In 1901 more than 26,000 people worked for the U.S. government in Washington. The city held universities, museums, and even a national zoo. But there was another side to the city.

Thousands of poor people—many of them African Americans—lived along narrow alleys in crowded, rundown buildings.

In 1917 the United States entered World War I. Thousands of workers moved to Washington to take jobs with the armed forces and the American Red Cross. There weren't enough houses and apartments for all the new residents. The U.S. government scrambled to quickly build lodgings.

About 10 years later, in 1929, an economic slump called the Great Depression hit the country. By 1932 one out of every four workers in the United States was unemployed.

During the Great Depression, many Washingtonians lived in poverty, without decent homes or indoor plumbing.

The Hunger Marchers

Three years after the depression began in 1929, nearly 13 million Americans were out of work. Many people couldn't afford to buy enough food to feed their families. Known as the Hunger Marchers, large groups of unemployed people came to Washington to ask the U.S. government for help. Within a year, the government responded with programs that put Americans back to work and offered help to the needy.

To help end the depression, the U.S. government designed programs to give people jobs. The government put people to work around the country, on projects such as road building and dam building. The government also needed thousands of workers to run the programs from Washington, D.C.

Most of the new government jobs went to white people. That's because, in the mid-1900s, most businesses and government offices would not hire African Americans. Many restaurants, hotels, and theaters refused to serve African Americans. Many colleges refused to allow African Americans to register for classes.

Unemployed men search for jobs during the Great Depression.

In 1939, because she was African American, singer Marian Anderson was not allowed to perform in Washington's Constitution Hall. First Lady Eleanor Roosevelt arranged for Anderson to sing at the Lincoln Memorial instead.

These forms of discrimination led black people to begin a wave of protests in Washington, D.C., and other U.S. cities. In July 1941, 50,000 black people planned to come to Washington to protest job discrimination—unfair hiring practices based on race. Before the march took place, President Franklin Roosevelt ordered the U.S. government to change its hiring practices.

In 1963 another huge crowd gathered at the Lincoln Memorial *(left)* to hear Martin Luther King Jr. *(above)* give a speech about freedom and equality. It would be remembered as King's "I Have a Dream" speech.

African Americans made more protests against discrimination. Their actions were known as the **civil rights movement.** In 1964 Congress passed the Civil Rights Act. This law forbids discrimination in public places such as hotels, parks, restaurants, and schools.

Civil rights marchers were just one group of U.S. citizens who came to Washington to express their views and to seek help from Congress. Throughout U.S. history, many different groups have come to the nation's capital to voice their feelings about many issues. In the 1960s and early 1970s, thousands of demonstrators came to Washington to protest U.S. involvement in the Vietnam War.

Over the years, many monuments and memorials have been built in Washington, D.C. These structures honor important individuals and groups in American history. They include the Washington Monument, the Lincoln Memorial, and the Vietnam Veterans Memorial.

In the 1990s, many people suggested that a new monument was needed—one to honor the veterans who fought for their country's freedom in World War II. In 1993 President Bill Clinton authorized construction of the National World War II Memorial, to be located on the National Mall between the Lincoln Memorial and the Washington Monument. Construction began in August 2001.

A distant view of the Lincoln Memorial *(left)*, the Washington Monument *(center)*, and the Capitol dome *(right)*

The Fight for Self-Governance

Washington, D.C., is not a U.S. state, so it does not have the kind of government that states have. It does not have a governor or ordinary senators and representatives. The city has a unique form of government.

The system has changed several times. In 1802 Congress decided that a city council and a mayor would run the city. At first, Washington residents could vote only for city council members. Later, they were allowed to elect the mayor. But people in Washington could not vote for president or vice president of the United States. They could not send representatives to Congress.

The system changed in 1874. Instead of an elected city council and mayor, Congress created a three-person government to run the district. The three officials were chosen by the U.S. president, not by the district residents.

In 1963 Washingtonians won the right to vote for president and vice president. In 1970 they gained the right to send a delegate to the House of Representatives. This person speaks on behalf of Washington, D.C., but is not allowed to vote like other representatives. In 1973

Washingtonians once again got the right to elect their own mayor and city council. But Congress can still pass laws for the city and can change decisions made by the city government.

In 1980 residents voted to make their city a state called New Columbia. Congress has not approved of statehood for Washington, D.C. In 1990 district residents began to send a "shadow delegation" to Congress. The three delegates try to convince lawmakers that New Columbia should be the 51st state.

In the city's first mayoral race in more than 100 years, Washingtonians elected Walter Washington as mayor in 1974.

On September 11, 2001, tragedy hit the nation's capital. Anti-American terrorists hijacked a passenger jet and crashed it into the Pentagon, headquarters of the U.S. military. The crash killed 189 people. At about the same time, terrorists flew two hijacked jets into the World Trade Center in New York City, killing more than 2,000 people there. Another hijacked plane crashed in Pennsylvania.

The U.S. government took action immediately. First, the military struck back against the terrorist leaders, who were hiding in Afghanistan. Government agents arrested terrorists working within the United States, and government agencies worked to improve security at airports and other public buildings. Throughout Washington, D.C., government officials are working together to keep Americans safe.

Workers reconstruct the section of the Pentagon that was damaged in the terrorist attack on September 11, 2001.

PEOPLE & ECONOMY

U.S.A. Headquarters

Washington, D.C., is home to about 572,000 residents. But the population of the entire metropolitan area is much larger—more than 4 million people. In the District of Columbia itself, almost two out of three people are African American—more than most other cities in the United States. In the suburbs, only about one out of five people are African American. Native Americans, Asian Americans, and Latinos make up a small percentage of the metropolitan area's population.

Young Washingtonians
enjoy a snowy winter.

Historic row houses line a street in Washington's Capitol Hill neighborhood.

Countries from around the world send representatives to Washington, D.C. Representatives from Canada work at the Canadian Embassy.

Washington is also home to more than 40,000 people who are citizens of other countries. Some of these people are ambassadors, who represent foreign countries. Others work for international organizations such as the World Bank, which lends money to countries around the world.

People who work for banks or government offices are called service workers, because they provide services to other people or businesses. Most of Washington's service workers hold jobs with the U.S. government. It is the largest employer in the Washington metropolitan area. About 370,000 people work for the U.S. government in the city and its suburbs.

Government employees do all kinds of jobs. Some work as managers, secretaries, or security guards at government offices. Employees at the Department of Defense direct the operations of the armed forces. Workers at the U.S. Postal Service oversee mail delivery and post offices around the country. The president of the United States and members of Congress work for the government, too.

Members of Congress are government service workers. They make laws for the United States.

Some workers in Washington **lobby,** or try to influence, Congress. Lobbyists work for specific groups of businesses, such as farmers or manufacturers. Lobbyists ask Congress to pass laws that will benefit their group members. Lobby organizations hire lawyers, bookkeepers, secretaries, and other workers to help get the job done.

Thousands more Washingtonians work in the tourist industry—at hotels, restaurants, and travel agencies. These workers offer services to the 20 million tourists who visit the capital city each year.

Other service workers in the capital include doctors, teachers, and salesclerks. Reporters are also service workers. They write articles for Washington's newspapers and magazines. *USA Today, National Geographic,* and *U.S. News & World Report* are some of the many well-known publications produced in Washington, D.C.

Some of Washington's workers help tourists find their way from place to place.

Thousands of Washingtonians hold construction jobs. They work on building roads, homes, and offices. Other workers have jobs in manufacturing. Many of these people work for printing and publishing companies, where they print magazines, pamphlets, and other materials.

Washington is known for its universities and colleges, which include Georgetown University, George Washington University, and American University. Howard University was founded in 1867 for the higher education of African Americans. Hearing-impaired students from all over the world come to study at Gallaudet University.

Statues of famous people are a common sight in Washington. This statue is being put into place by construction workers.

The Vietnam Veterans Memorial
lists the names of all Americans
who were killed during the war.

Students, residents, and tourists all
enjoy Washington's many attractions.
Some of the city's most popular sights are
the Capitol building, the White House,
the Washington Monument, the Lincoln
Memorial, and the headquarters of the
Federal Bureau of Investigation (FBI).

Visitors to the National Archives can
see historical documents such as the U.S.
Constitution, the Bill of Rights, and the
Declaration of Independence. These
valuable old papers are displayed in
bronze and glass cases. In case of fire
or another emergency, the cases can be
lowered quickly into a special vault. Tourists also
enjoy watching sheets of dollar bills and postage
stamps roll off giant presses at the Bureau of
Engraving and Printing.

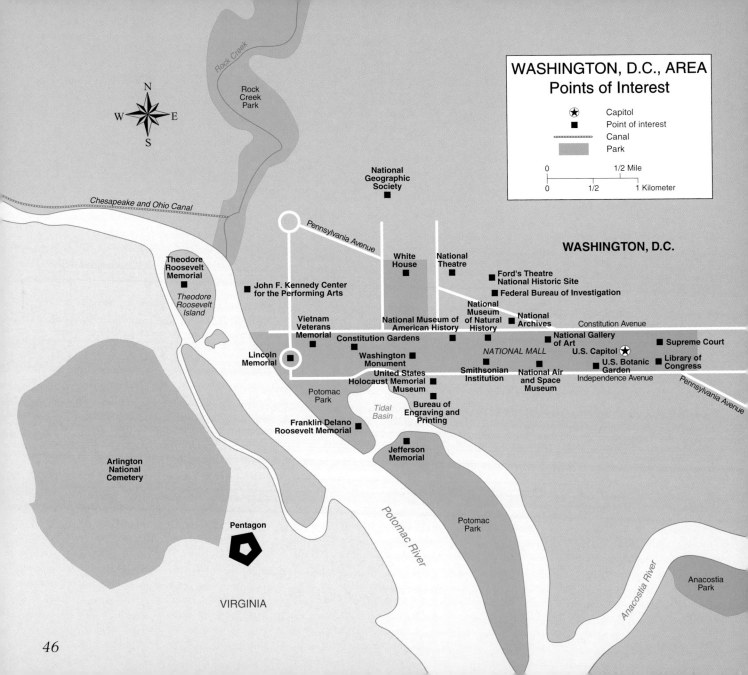

WASHINGTON, D.C., AREA
Points of Interest

⊛ Capitol
■ Point of interest
⸬⸬⸬ Canal
▨ Park

0   1/2 Mile
0   1/2   1 Kilometer

Rock Creek

Rock Creek Park

N
W E
S

Chesapeake and Ohio Canal

National Geographic Society

WASHINGTON, D.C.

Pennsylvania Avenue

Theodore Roosevelt Memorial

Theodore Roosevelt Island

John F. Kennedy Center for the Performing Arts

White House

National Theatre

Ford's Theatre National Historic Site

Federal Bureau of Investigation

Vietnam Veterans Memorial

National Museum of American History

National Museum of Natural History

National Archives

National Gallery of Art

Constitution Avenue

Lincoln Memorial

Constitution Gardens

NATIONAL MALL

U.S. Capitol ⊛

Supreme Court

Washington Monument

Smithsonian Institution

National Air and Space Museum

U.S. Botanic Garden

Library of Congress

United States Holocaust Memorial Museum

Independence Avenue

Pennsylvania Avenue

Potomac Park

Tidal Basin

Bureau of Engraving and Printing

Franklin Delano Roosevelt Memorial

Jefferson Memorial

Arlington National Cemetery

Potomac Park

Potomac River

Pentagon

VIRGINIA

Anacostia River

Anacostia Park

46

For lovers of museums and the arts, Washington, D.C., is a treasure trove. The Smithsonian Institution includes many museums, such as the National Gallery of Art and the National Air and Space Museum. Hundreds of priceless paintings hang in the art museum. The National Air and Space Museum features airplanes, rockets, and space capsules and exhibits about the history of air and space travel.

Aviation buffs can visit the National Air and Space Museum.

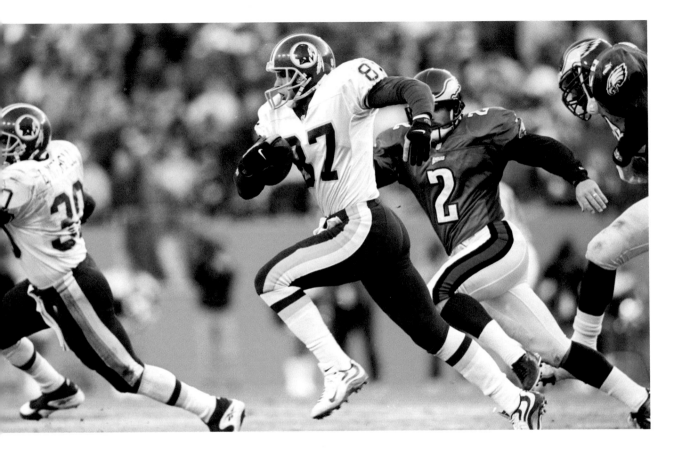

Football fans in the capital like watching the Redskins.

Theatergoers attend plays at the National Theatre, Ford's Theatre, and Arena Stage. Concerts at the John F. Kennedy Center for the Performing Arts also draw big audiences. Sports fans watch the Washington Redskins football team play in

FedExField. Fans also enjoy watching the
Washington Wizards basketball team shoot hoops
and the Washington Capitals hockey team pass the
puck in the MCI Center.

The Chesapeake and Ohio Canal National
Historical Park attracts outdoor enthusiasts. The
canal, which runs more than 180 miles from
Georgetown to Cumberland, Maryland, was built in
the early 1800s to haul tons of coal to Washington.
Visitors can travel along the canal the way coal
once did—in boats pulled by mules that walk along
the waterway. The path beside the
canal is also a popular place to hike
or ride bicycles.

A boat moves down the
Chesapeake and Ohio Canal
the old-fashioned way—
pulled by mules.

Horseback riding is only one of the many activities available at Rock Creek Park.

Rock Creek Park, which houses the National Zoological Park, is one of the largest woodland city parks in the world. The zoo's most famous resident was Hsing-Hsing, a giant panda given to the United

States by the People's Republic of China in 1972. Hsing-Hsing died in 1999, but two new young pandas, Mei Xiang and Tian Tian, arrived at the zoo from China in 2000.

From its theaters and museums to its hiking trails and sports arenas, Washington, D.C., is just what a capital city should be—a place with something to interest everyone.

The pandas are some of the most popular animals at the National Zoological Park.

THE ENVIRONMENT

The War on CFCs

bout 70 percent of the people who live in Washington's metropolitan area drive cars to and from work. On hot and muggy summer days, many drivers count on their car air conditioners to make the ride more comfortable. But the air conditioners add to a serious environmental problem—the destruction of the **ozone** layer above the earth.

Ozone, a type of oxygen, forms a layer in the upper atmosphere, high above the earth's surface. The ozone layer is important because it absorbs most of the sun's **ultraviolet (UV) radiation.** In large doses, UV radiation can cause skin cancer and other health problems in humans. It can harm and even kill plants and animals. UV radiation can also make

paint crack more easily and can make plastics, rubber, and building materials wear out sooner than they normally would.

Washington is a crowded city with lots of car traffic.

In 1985 scientists discovered that the ozone layer over Antarctica (the continent at the South Pole) thins dramatically every spring. Three years later,

Earth Probe TOMS Total Ozone September 16, 2000

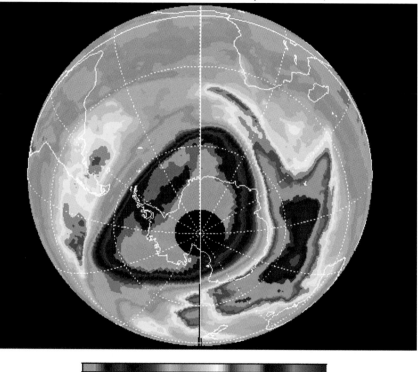

<120   200   280   360   440   520>
Ozone (Dobson Units)

This satellite picture shows that the ozone level is thinning over Antarctica. Areas of dark blue, purple, pink, and gray have low levels of ozone.

in 1988, researchers announced that the ozone layer over the entire planet was thinning faster than previously thought.

Chemicals called **chlorofluorocarbons (CFCs)** are the main substances that harm the ozone layer. These chemicals are used to make a number of products, including refrigerators and air conditioners. When CFCs escape from products into the upper atmosphere, they destroy ozone. When this happens, more UV radiation reaches the earth, threatening humans, plants, and animals.

UV radiation can harm people, animals, and plants, including Washington's famous cherry trees.

CFCs can leak out of car air conditioners during repair jobs.

Car air conditioners contain more CFCs than most other products. Even in good condition, car air conditioners leak CFCs. The chemicals can also escape during auto accidents and when air conditioners are being repaired.

Together with the governments of many other countries, the U.S. government is working to protect the ozone layer. In 1987 the United States and about 80 other nations signed an agreement called the Montreal Protocol. By signing this document, the participating nations agreed to cut CFC production in half by 1998. In 1990 the countries signed an addition to the document. They agreed to stop making CFCs altogether by the year 2000. By 1996 most countries, including the United States, had complied with the agreement.

Congress has passed additional laws to make sure that CFCs manufactured before the Montreal Protocol don't harm the ozone layer. For instance, one law says that CFCs in old refrigerators and air conditioners must be captured before the items are thrown away. The CFCs can then be recycled.

New laws have helped cut levels of CFCs escaping from cars into the air.

By walking and biking instead of driving cars, people can help protect the ozone layer.

But the new laws are hard to enforce. Sometimes people throw out old air conditioners and refrigerators without capturing the CFCs. And the equipment needed to capture and recycle CFCs is expensive. Even if everyone follows the law, the ozone layer will not be safe for many years. Once CFCs escape into the upper atmosphere, they can destroy ozone for up to 100 years.

Getting rid of CFCs depends partly on ordinary people. Car owners in Washington, D.C., and other parts of the United States can help by asking their auto mechanics to recycle CFCs. People who buy old cars can choose ones without air conditioners. Newer cars have become safer for the environment. In the 1990s, automakers started producing car air conditioners that don't contain CFCs.

Even if you don't own a car, you can help save the ozone layer. By writing to the politicians from your state, you can try to persuade Congress to pass laws that reduce air pollution. Together, the U.S. government in Washington and all of the nation's citizens can make the earth a healthier place to live.

Fun Facts

Washington, D.C., is one of the few cities in the world that was planned before it was built.

Rising 555 feet into the air, the Washington Monument is the tallest building in Washington, D.C. When the tower first opened in 1888, the elevator ride to the top took 10 minutes. Now the ride takes only 70 seconds.

The Library of Congress is the world's largest library. With almost 121 million items, the library's collection includes books, manuscripts, newspapers, musical scores, maps, microfilm, photos, recordings, and films.

The White House is the residence of the president of the United States.

During the War of 1812, many government buildings—including the president's house—were burned. As part of the repair job, the president's fireblackened residence was painted white. It has been called the White House ever since.

Abraham Lincoln, the 16th president of the United States, was shot at Ford's Theatre on April 14, 1865. Visitors to Washington, D.C., can tour the theater and the house across the street where the president died the next day.

Martin Luther King Jr. gave his famous "I Have a Dream" speech at the Lincoln Memorial on August 28, 1963. More than 200,000 Americans listened to King's speech, which was part of a famous march on Washington for civil rights.

George Washington, a skilled mason, laid the cornerstone for the U.S. Capitol in 1793.

OFFICIAL SONG

Washington, D.C., does not have its own official song. But Washingtonians who wish to celebrate their city in song might choose the U.S. national anthem.

THE STAR-SPANGLED BANNER

Words by Francis Scott Key; music traditional

You can hear "The Star-Spangled Banner" by visiting the official White House website: <http://www.whitehouse.gov/national-anthem/usa-full.html>

A WASHINGTON, D.C., RECIPE

Starting in 1912, Japan sent thousands of cherry trees to Washington, D.C., as a gift to the United States. The cherry trees are still one of the most famous sights in Washington, especially when they bloom in spring. Every year, Washington holds a Cherry Blossom Festival to celebrate the beautiful spring blossoms. You can celebrate the cherry trees year-round by making cherry lemonade.

CHERRY LEMONADE

1¾ cups freshly squeezed lemon juice (from about 12 lemons)
1 cup sugar
3 quarts cold water
1 pound fresh cherries, with pits and stems removed

1. In a gallon container, combine lemon juice and sugar.
2. Stir the mixture until the sugar is dissolved.
3. Pour in the water.
4. Add the cherries.
5. Stir until blended.
6. Pour into ice-filled glasses and serve.

Makes 6 to 8 servings.

HISTORICAL TIMELINE

1600 Piscataway, Powhatan, and Nanticoke Indians live in the region that later becomes the Washington, D.C., area.

1791 George Washington chooses the site for the nation's capital; Pierre Charles L'Enfant creates a plan for the city.

1800 The federal government moves to Washington from a temporary capital in Philadelphia.

1814 British troops burn U.S. government buildings during the War of 1812.

1846 The Smithsonian Institution is created.

1865 Abraham Lincoln is assassinated at Ford's Theatre.

1885 The Washington Monument is opened.

1912 Japan sends a gift of cherry trees to Washington, D.C.

1922 The Lincoln Memorial is opened.

1930s The U.S. government creates thousands of new jobs to fight the Great Depression. Many of the jobs are in Washington.

1939 Singer Marian Anderson performs at the Lincoln Memorial.

1943 The Jefferson Memorial is opened.

1963 Martin Luther King Jr. gives his "I Have a Dream" speech at the Lincoln Memorial.

1970 The U.S. Congress passes a law allowing Washington to have a delegate in the U.S. House of Representatives.

1973 Washingtonians can elect local officials for the first time in 100 years.

1982 The Vietnam Veterans Memorial is completed.

1990 Sharon Pratt Kelly is elected mayor of Washington. She is the first African American woman to serve as mayor of a major U.S. city.

1991 Washington, D.C., marks its 200th anniversary as the nation's capital.

2001 Construction begins on the National World War II Memorial.

2001 Terrorists crash a hijacked passenger plane into the Pentagon, killing 189 people. The attack is part of a major terrorist strike against the United States.

OUTSTANDING WASHINGTONIANS

Elgin Baylor

Ann Beattie

Billie Burke

Connie Chung

Edward Franklin Albee III (born 1928) is an award-winning playwright from Washington, D.C. Among his best-known works are *Who's Afraid of Virginia Woolf?*, *A Delicate Balance*, and *Seascape.*

Elgin Baylor (born 1934) played basketball with both the Minneapolis Lakers and the Los Angeles Lakers. Born in Washington, D.C., Baylor became vice president of basketball operations for the Los Angeles Clippers in 1986.

Ann Beattie (born 1947) writes novels and short stories. Born in Washington, D.C., Beattie has contributed stories to well-known literary magazines such as the *New Yorker* and *Harper's.* In 1985 she wrote a book called *Spectacles* for young readers. Her novels include *Falling in Place* and *Picturing Will.*

Billie Burke (1885–1970) was born into a family of entertainers in Washington, D.C. A talented actress, Burke was well known for her roles on stage and in films. Her most famous role was that of Glinda the Good Witch in *The Wizard of Oz.*

Connie Chung (born 1946), an award-winning broadcast journalist, was born in Washington, D.C. Since the 1980s, she has anchored various news programs for NBC, CBS, and ABC.

Benjamin O. Davis Jr. (born 1912), a U.S. Air Force officer, was born in Washington, D.C. In 1959 he became the first black officer in American history to earn the rank of major general. He was promoted to lieutenant general in 1965. His father, Benjamin O. Davis, served as a brigadier general in the army during World War II.

Duke Ellington (1899–1974) was born in Washington, D.C. A piano player, Ellington became one of the most famous jazz composers and bandleaders of his time. He wrote more than 5,000 original works, including "Mood Indigo" and "Sophisticated Lady."

Duke Ellington

Marvin Gaye (1939–1984), a singer and songwriter, was the son of a Washington minister. Gaye began his career singing with the choir at his father's church. Gaye's hits include "I Heard It through the Grapevine" and "What's Going On."

Marvin Gaye

Albert "Al" Gore Jr. (born 1948), vice president of the United States from 1993 to 2001, was born in Washington, D.C. In 2000 Gore ran for president of the United States but lost to George W. Bush. Before serving as vice president, Gore was a Democratic senator from Tennessee.

Goldie Hawn (born 1945) is an actress and movie producer. She was born in Washington, D.C., and grew up in Takoma Park, Maryland. From 1968 to 1970, Hawn appeared in the TV comedy *Rowan & Martin's Laugh In.* She has acted in many movies, including *Cactus Flower* and *Bird on a Wire.*

Albert "Al" Gore Jr.

Helen Hayes (1900–1993), a native of Washington, D.C., began her acting career when she was only five years old. As an adult, she acted in Broadway plays and starred in many films, including *Airport*, for which she won an Oscar in 1970.

J. Edgar Hoover (1895–1972) was a lawyer and public official born in Washington, D.C. Hoover began working for the U.S. Department of Justice in 1917. In 1924 he became director of the Federal Bureau of Investigation and served in that position until his death in 1972.

Helen Hayes

William Hurt

William Hurt (born 1950) is a well-known stage and film actor. He has starred in numerous movies, including *The Big Chill*, *Broadcast News*, and *The Doctor*. In 1985 Hurt won an Oscar for his performance in *Kiss of the Spider Woman*. Hurt is from Washington, D.C.

Samuel L. Jackson (born 1948) is an accomplished Hollywood actor from Washington, D.C. He has appeared in dozens of feature films, including *Jackie Brown*, *Pulp Fiction*, and *Jurassic Park*.

Samuel L. Jackson

John F. Kennedy Jr. (1960–1999) was the son of President John F. Kennedy. Born in Washington, D.C., Kennedy founded the political magazine *George* in 1995. In 1999 Kennedy, his wife, and his wife's sister were killed when a plane he was piloting crashed into the ocean off the coast of Massachusetts.

Sugar Ray Leonard (born 1956) is a former boxer known for his speed and clever footwork. Born into a family of boxers, Leonard won a gold medal at the 1976 Olympic Games. During his professional career, he won world championship titles in five weight classifications. Leonard is from Washington, D.C.

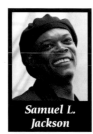

John F. Kennedy Jr.

Roger Mudd (born 1928), a journalist from Washington, D.C., has won several Emmy Awards for his work as a reporter. Mudd has worked as a correspondent for a number of TV networks. His career has spanned more than 40 years.

Eleanor Holmes Norton (born 1937) is an African American lawyer and government official. Born in Washington, D.C., Norton worked as a lawyer for the American Civil Liberties Union from 1965 to 1970. She later taught law at Georgetown University. Since 1991 Norton has been the District of Columbia's nonvoting delegate to Congress.

Sugar Ray Leonard

Norman F. Ramsey (born 1915) is a Washington-born physicist who did important research into the properties of atoms and molecules. Ramsey received the Nobel Prize in physics in 1989.

Marjorie Kinnan Rawlings (1896–1953) was born in Washington, D.C. Rawlings gave up a career as a journalist to live on a farm in rural Florida, where she began to write fiction. Her best-known book, *The Yearling*, earned her a Pulitzer Prize in 1939.

Marjorie Kinnan Rawlings

Chita Rivera (born 1933) is a famous actress, singer, and dancer known for her work on Broadway. Rivera starred in the Broadway hits *West Side Story* and *Bye Bye Birdie*, and won Tony Awards for her roles in *The Rink* and *Kiss of the Spider Woman*. Rivera is from Washington, D.C.

John Philip Sousa (1854–1932) was a famous bandleader and composer born in Washington, D.C. Known as the March King, Sousa wrote more than 100 march tunes. His most famous work is "The Stars and Stripes Forever," a popular patriotic march.

John Philip Sousa

Jean Toomer (1894–1967) was an African American writer of poetry and prose. He is best known for *Cane* (1923), a book that mixed poetry and stories to depict the lives of African Americans. Toomer was born in Washington, D.C. He was part of the Harlem Renaissance, an African American literary movement of the 1920s.

Jean Toomer

Gore Vidal (born 1929) is a popular novelist, playwright, and essayist. His works of fiction include *Williwaw*, *The City and the Pillar*, and *Myra Breckinridge*. Vidal was raised in the house of his grandfather, U.S. senator Thomas Gore, in Washington, D.C.

Gore Vidal

FACTS-AT-A-GLANCE

Nicknames: Nation's Capital, Capital City

Motto: Justitia Omnibus (Justice for All)

Flower: American beauty rose

Tree: scarlet oak

Bird: wood thrush

Founded: 1791

City area: 68 square miles

Average January temperature: 37° F

Average July temperature: 78° F

City population: 572,059 (2000 census)

U.S. senators: 0

U.S. representatives: 1 (does not vote)

Electoral votes: 3

The Washington, D.C., flag is based on the coat of arms, or official emblem, used by George Washington's family. The flag was designed in 1938.

POPULATION GROWTH

Thousands

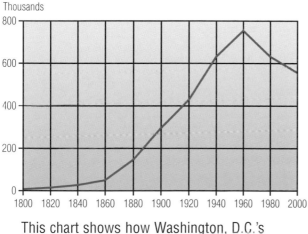

This chart shows how Washington, D.C.'s population has changed from 1800 to 2000.

Washington's official seal shows the figure of Justice placing a wreath on a statue of George Washington.

WHERE WASHINGTONIANS WORK

Services—69 percent (services includes jobs in trade; community, social, and personal services; finance, insurance, and real estate; transportation, communication, and utilities)

Government—21 percent

Construction—6 percent

Manufacturing—4 percent

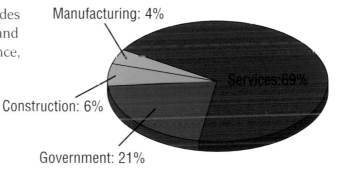

Manufacturing: 4%

Construction: 6%

Government: 21%

Services: 69%

MAJOR PARKS AND GARDENS

Anacostia Park, Kenilworth Avenue

With over 1,200 acres, Anacostia is one of the city's largest recreation areas. Kenilworth Park and Aquatic Gardens is located here, along with a golf course and marinas.

Chesapeake and Ohio Canal National Historical Park, 1057 Thomas Jefferson Street N.W.

The C&O Canal stretches 184 miles from Georgetown to Cumberland, Maryland. Bikers, hikers, and joggers can travel the pathways along the canal, while canoers and kayakers can paddle on the water.

Constitution Gardens, 17th Street and Constitution Avenue N.W.

This 45-acre park in the National Mall features a 6-acre lake, walking and biking paths, picnic areas, and more than 2,500 shade trees.

Kenilworth Park and Aquatic Gardens, Douglas Street and Anacostia Avenue N.E.

This park has nearly 12 acres of aquatic gardens, featuring dozens of species of plants and flowers. Frogs, turtles, and water birds also make their homes here.

National Arboretum, 3501 New York Avenue N.E.

Opened in 1927, the arboretum contains 415 acres of plants and trees from around the world. Special features include the National Bonsai and Penjing Museum, the Native Plant Collection, the Conifer Collection, and the Friendship Garden.

Potomac Park, Ohio Drive S.W.

Divided into East and West Potomac Parks, this site covers more than 328 acres. The park holds the Jefferson Memorial and the Tidal Basin, as well as many recreational facilities. Thousands of cherry trees bloom here in spring.

Rock Creek Park, 3545 Williamsburg Lane N.W.

Rock Creek Park covers nearly 2,000 acres of rolling hills, woods, and meadows. Rock Creek runs through the center of the park, along with many trails for hikers, bikers, and horseback riders. The National Zoological Park is also located here.

Theodore Roosevelt Island, in the Potomac River off the George Washington Parkway

Created in honor of the 26th president, the island offers nature trail and tours. It also contains a memorial to President Roosevelt.

U.S. Botanic Garden, National Mall between Maryland Avenue and C Street

Established in 1820, this is the oldest botanic garden in North America. Facilities include the Conservatory, Bartholdi Park, and the National Garden.

The U.S. Botanic Garden Conservatory

PLACES TO VISIT

Bureau of Engraving and Printing, 14th and C Streets S.W.
The bureau is in charge of designing, engraving, and printing paper currency. Visitors can see millions of dollars being made from large sheets of paper into wallet-ready bills.

Explorers Hall at the National Geographic Society, 1145 17th Street N.W.
This museum features *Geographica*, an interactive exhibit about the earth and its inhabitants. Earth Station One is an amphitheater that lets you feel what it's like to orbit in space.

Ford's Theatre, 511 10th Street N.W.
The site of Lincoln's assassination, the theater offers musicals and plays that highlight American life and culture. It also displays items related to Lincoln's life and the assassination. Peterson House, where Lincoln died, is across the street.

Library of Congress, 10 First Street S.E.
The world's largest library holds about 121 million items in three buildings. Visitors can see original historical documents, such as a Gutenberg Bible from the 1450s, Abraham Lincoln's Gettysburg Address, and Mathew Brady's Civil War photographs.

National Air and Space Museum, Seventh Street and Independence Avenue S.W.
Part of the Smithsonian Institution, the museum displays airplanes flown by Orville Wright and Charles Lindbergh. Other exhibits teach about spacecraft and space travel.

National Mall, between Constitution and Independence Avenues S.W.

This splendid park runs about two miles from the Capitol to the Washington Monument. The Mall is surrounded by important buildings and monuments, including the National Archives, the Vietnam Veterans Memorial, and the U.S. Botanic Garden.

National Zoological Park, 3001 Connecticut Avenue N.W.

Here visitors can see birds and animals from all over the world, including the panda bears Mei Xiang and Tian Tian from China.

U.S. Capitol, Capitol Hill

Senators and representatives meet at the Capitol to make laws for the nation. Visitors can tour the magnificent building, which contains beautiful sculptures, paintings, and furnishings.

Vietnam Veterans Memorial, Constitution Avenue and Henry Bacon Drive N.W.

This black granite wall is inscribed with the names of the 58,209 Americans missing or killed during the Vietnam War. A life-size bronze sculpture depicts three servicemen in Vietnam.

Washington Monument, 15th St. and Constitution Avenue N.W.

This majestic tower, opened in 1885, honors the first president of the United States. Visitors can take elevator rides to the top of the 555-foot monument for a spectacular view.

White House, 1600 Pennsylvania Avenue N.W.

The White House has served as the home of every American president except George Washington. It also serves as the president's office. Five rooms are open for public touring.

ANNUAL EVENTS

Martin Luther King Jr. Celebration—*January*

Chinese New Year Celebration—*February*

Smithsonian Kite Festival—*March*

National Cherry Blossom Festival—*March–April*

White House Easter Egg Roll—*April*

Memorial Day Weekend—*May*

Festival of American Folklife—*June*

Independence Day—*July*

National Frisbee Festival—*September*

Taste of D.C.—*October*

National Christmas Tree Lighting—*December*

LEARN MORE ABOUT WASHINGTON, D.C.

BOOKS

Elish, Dan. *Washington, D.C.* Tarrytown, NY: Marshall Cavendish, 1998. For older readers.

Stein, R. Conrad. *Washington, D.C.* Danbury, CT: Children's Press, 1999.

Thompson, Kathleen. *Washington, D.C.* Austin: Raintree/Steck-Vaughn, 1996.

Special Interest

Andryszewski, Tricia. *The March on Washington 1963: Gathering to Be Heard.* Brookfield, CT: Millbrook Press, 1996. Through words and photographs, this book tells the story of the civil rights march of 1963, when thousands gathered in Washington, and Martin Luther King Jr. delivered his famous "I Have a Dream" speech.

Ashabranner, Brent. *Their Names to Live: What the Vietnam Veterans Memorial Means to America.* Brookfield, CT: Twenty-First Century Books, 1998. Nearly 60,000 names are inscribed on the memorial to America's Vietnam veterans. This book tells how the memorial was created and describes its impact on soldiers' families and friends.

Bay, Ann Phillips. *A Kids' Guide to the Smithsonian.* Washington, D.C.: Smithsonian Institution Press, 1996. With 140 million items in its collection, the Smithsonian is one of the world's greatest museums. This book introduces readers to the institution, its most popular museums, its history, and its many treasures.

Ransom, Candice F. *George Washington.* Minneapolis, MN: Lerner Publications Company, 2002. George Washington never lived in the city that bears his name, but he chose the city's location, oversaw city planning, and laid the cornerstone for the Capitol. This book tells the story of our nation's first president.

Fiction

Harness, Cheryl. *Ghosts of the White House.* New York: Simon & Schuster, 1998. Bored by the White House tour guide, Sara encounters the ghost of George Washington, who gives her an insider's tour of presidential history.

Reeder, Carolyn. *Captain Kate.* New York: William Morrow & Co., 1999. While the Civil War rages around them, 12-year-old Kate and her stepbrother, Seth, pilot their family's boat along the C&O Canal from Cumberland, Maryland, to Washington, D.C.

Robinet, Harriette Gillem. *Washington City Is Burning.* New York: Simon & Schuster, 1996. Twelve-year-old Virginia, a slave, is sent to work for President James Madison and his wife, Dolley, in the White House. There, she not only witnesses the burning of Washington during the War of 1812 but also helps guide runaway slaves to safety.

WEBSITES

Welcome to Washington, District of Columbia

http://www.washingtondc.gov

The district's official website provides information on city government, business, news, and community services.

Washington, D.C.: The American Experience

http://www.Washington.org

This site offers everything the tourist needs to plan a Washington, D.C., vacation, including information on dining, lodging, special events, sightseeing, transportation, and history.

Welcome to the White House

http://www.whitehouse.gov

This site gives visitors an introduction to the president, the White House building, and the job of running the government. A special kids' section includes quizzes, cartoons, and other fun stuff.

The Washington Post

http://washpost.com

One of the nation's leading papers, the *Washington Post* offers lots of national political news, as well as local information about business, entertainment, community events, and city government.

Smithsonian Institution

http://www.si.edu

This great museum complex includes many smaller museums, galleries, archives, and research centers. From the Smithsonian's home page, visitors can follow links to related organizations.

PRONUNCIATION GUIDE

Anacostia (an-uh-KAHS-tee-uh)

Bladensburg (BLAY-duhnz-burg)

Chesapeake (CHEHS-uh-peek)

Gallaudet (gal-uh-DEHT)

L'Enfant, Pierre Charles (lahn-FAHNt, pee-AIR CHAHRLZ)

Manassas (muh-NAS-uhs)

Nanticoke (NAN-tih-kohk)

Piedmont (PEED-mahnt)

Piscataway (pihs-KAT-uh-way)

Potomac (puh-TOH-mihk)

Powhatan (pow-uh-TAN)

The U.S. flag waves proudly in front of the Washington Monument.

GLOSSARY

abolitionist: a person who works to abolish, or end, something. The term usually refers to the people who worked to abolish slavery before the Civil War.

chlorofluorocarbons (CFCs): a group of chemicals that contain chlorine, fluorine, and carbon. CFCs are used as cooling agents in air conditioners and refrigerators. In the upper atmosphere, CFCs destroy the earth's protective ozone layer.

civil rights movement: a movement to gain equal rights, or freedoms, for all citizens—regardless of race, religion, or sex

lobby: to try to persuade lawmakers to pass laws that will benefit a certain group, company, or organization

ozone: a gas found in the earth's upper atmosphere, about 9 to 18 miles above the earth's surface. Ozone in the upper atmosphere shields the earth from harmful rays from the sun.

precipitation: rain, snow, and other forms of moisture that fall to the earth

treaty: an agreement between two or more groups, usually having to do with peace or trade

ultraviolet (UV) radiation: an invisible form of light released by the sun. In large doses, UV radiation can cause serious health problems.

INDEX

PHOTO ACKNOWLEDGMENTS

Cover photographs by © Ric Ergenbright/CORBIS (left) and © Dallas and John Heaton/CORBIS (right); PresentationMaps.com, pp. 1, 8, 46; © James P. Blair/CORBIS, pp. 2–3; © Ron Watts/CORBIS, p. 3; Anne B. Keiser, pp. 4, 7 (inset), 17 (inset), 38 (inset), 52 (inset), 55; Mae Scanlan, pp. 6, 12, 38 (left), 44; Gene Ahrens, pp. 9, 35; © Joseph Sohm; Visions of America/CORBIS, pp. 10–11; Saul Mayer, pp. 13, 15; Jerry Hennen, p. 16; Library of Congress, pp. 17, 18, 20, 21, 24, 26, 27, 28 (both), 29, 30, 32; National Park Service, pp. 19, 43; © Bettmann/CORBIS, pp. 22, 23, 33 (right), 36, 68 (bottom), 69 (second from bottom); *Dictionary of American Portraits*, p. 25 (top); Washington, D.C., Convention and Visitors Assoc., p. 25 (bottom); National Archives, pp. 31 (#69-N-17200), 33 (left); © Jay Mallin, pp. 37, 39, 42, 51, 57, 73; Colette Champagne, p. 40; Richard Day, pp. 45, 47; © ALLSPORT USA/Jamie Squire, p. 48; Thomas Henion, pp. 49, 80; © Kelly-Mooney Photography/CORBIS, p. 50; Corbis Royalty Free Images, p. 53; NASA, p. 54; Wendy W. Cortesi, p. 56; Frederica Georgia, p. 58; George Karn, p. 60; The White House, p. 61; Tim Seeley, pp. 63, 71 (top left, bottom); Wen Roberts, p. 66 (top); Benjamin Ford, p. 66 (second from top); Hollywood Book & Poster, pp. 66 (second from bottom), 67 (top, second from top, bottom), 68 (top), 69 (second from top); © Mitchell Gerber/CORBIS, pp. 66 (bottom), 68 (second from bottom); Independent Picture Service, p. 67 (second from bottom); © Reuters NewMedia Inc./CORBIS, pp. 68 (second from top), 69 (bottom); University of Florida, Dept. of Special Collections, p. 69 (top); Jean Matheny, p. 70 (top).